ELLIOTT CARTER

FIGMENT VI

for solo oboe

HENDON MUSIC

BOOSEY & HAWKES

AN IMAGEM COMPANY

DISTRIBUTED BY

HAL•LEONARD®
CORPORATION
7777 W. BLUEMOUND RD. P.O. BOX 13819 MILWAUKEE, WI 53213

www.boosey.com
www.halleonard.com

COMPOSER'S NOTE

Figment VI was written for Heinz Holliger's brilliant command of
his instrument, and I tried to express my gratitude for his performances.

–Elliott Carter

ANMERKUNG DES KOMPONISTEN

Figment VI wurde für Heinz Holliger geschrieben, der sein Instrument so
meisterlich beherrscht. Ich versuchte hiermit meine Dankbarkeit für seine
musikalische Leistung zum Ausdruck zu bringen.

–Elliott Carter

NOTE DU COMPOSITEUR

Figment VI a été écrit pour la magnifique maitrise qu'Heinz Holliger a de
son instrument, et j'ai tenté d'exprimer ma gratitude pour ses interprétations.

–Elliott Carter

FIGMENT VI
to Heinz

for Oboe

Elliott Carter
(2011)

NYC 11/30/11